Chocolate Satisfaction

FOR DESPERATE HOUSEWIVES

EDITED BY SARAH ARAK

Introduction

CHOCOLATE IS PERHAPS THE SEXIEST FOOD IN EXISTENCE.
Smooth in texture, intense in taste, subtly perfumed and visually elegant, chocolate is a rich source of sensory pleasure—one that we have all adored for centuries. The very act of unwrapping chocolate is a tempting experience, not unlike the first feast of intimacy. Our passion for chocolate might be explained by the fact that we derive such pleasure not only from the act of eating chocolate, but also from the anticipation of doing so. Perhaps that is why chocolate is so adored by desperate, desirable, and often bored, housewives.

It's therefore no surprise that chocolate is so often described in passionate terms. Aside from its overt sensual properties, chocolate is also known for its exciting psychoactive effects, which are said to mirror those of falling in love. In fact, the celebrated Italian libertine Giacomo Casanova (1725–1798) was said to serve women hot chocolate like champagne.

As the demand for chocolate spread throughout the world in the late 1700s, a heated controversy ensued over whether chocolate was good or evil. A Spanish monk believed the temptatious substance was diabolical, and that its "invigorating properties were the work of evil spirits."

Say what you will about chocolate, women, and especially desperate and desirable housewives, love it. We eat it for comfort and energy, give and receive it as gifts, and enjoy it as both a substitute for love and as enhancement of it. Chocolate is that rare something that tempts us, indeed, to feel alive and satisfied.

I NEVER RESIST TEMPTATION, BECAUSE

I HAVE FOUND THAT THINGS WHICH

ARE BAD FOR ME DO NOT TEMPT ME.

—William Shakespeare,
The Tragedy of King Richard the Third
(King Richard at IV, ii)

THOSE WHO FLEE TEMPTATION

GENERALLY LEAVE A

FORWARDING ADDRESS.

—Lane Olinghouse

FOR TO TEMPT AND TO BE TEMPTED ARE THINGS

VERY NEARLY ALLIED...WHENEVER FEELING HAS

ANYTHING TO DO IN THE MATTER, NO SOONER

IS IT EXCITED THAN WE HAVE ALREADY GONE

VASTLY FARTHER THAN WE ARE AWARE OF.

—Catherine the Great
(Empress of Russia, 1729–1796)

RESIST NO TEMPTATION:

A GUILTY CONSCIENCE IS MORE

HONORABLE THAN REGRET.

—Author Unknown

Do you really think it is weakness that yields to temptation? I tell you that there are terrible temptations which it requires strength and courage to yield to.

—Oscar Wilde (Irish poet, novelist, dramatist and critic, 1854–1900)

THE TROUBLE WITH RESISTING

TEMPTATION IS THAT IT MAY NEVER

COME YOUR WAY AGAIN.

—Korman's Law

IF YOU'RE GOING TO DO SOMETHING TONIGHT

THAT YOU'LL BE SORRY FOR

TOMORROW MORNING...SLEEP LATE.

—Henny Youngman
(American humorist, 1906–1998)

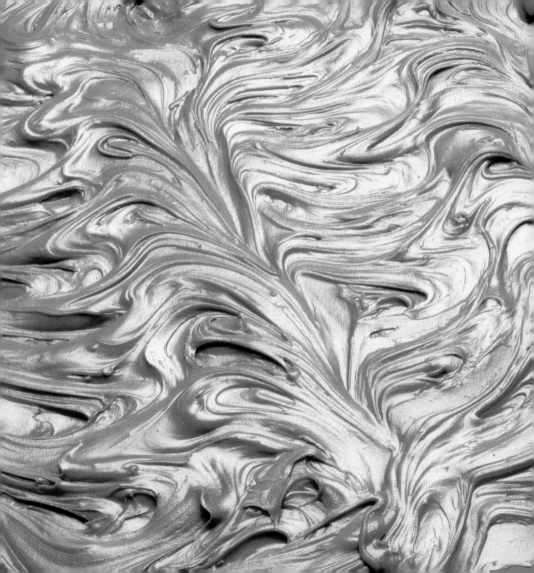

Every now and then, a woman

has to indulge herself.

—Author Unknown

SELF-DISCIPLINE IMPLIES SOME

UNPLEASANT THINGS TO ME, INCLUDING

STAYING AWAY FROM CHOCOLATE.

—Oleg Kiselev
(Russian guitarist, composer, b. 1964)

Ever notice that the whisper

of temptation can be heard farther

than the loudest call to duty?

—Earl Wilson
(American journalist, 1907–1987)

WE USUALLY KNOW WHAT WE CAN DO,

BUT TEMPTATION SHOW US WHO WE ARE.

—Thomas Kempis
(Ascetical writer, c. 1380–1471)

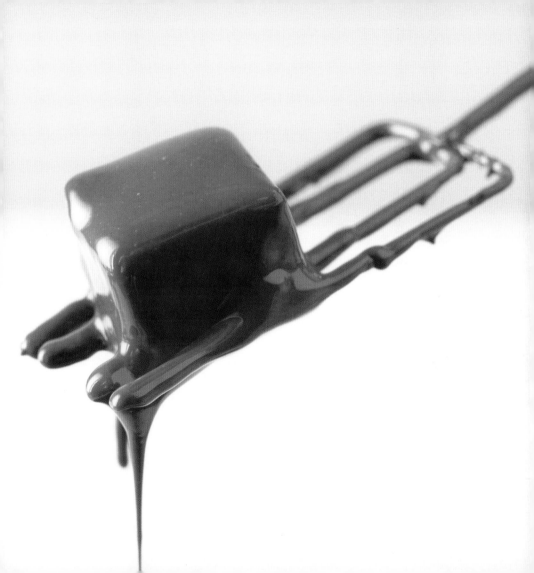

I T'S NOT THE HAVING,

IT'S THE GETTING.

—Elizabeth Taylor
(American actress, b. 1932)

THE LAST TEMPTATION IS THE

GREATEST TREASON: TO DO THE RIGHT

DEED FOR THE WRONG REASON.

—T.S. Eliot (American-born writer
and poet, 1888–1965)

TEMPTATION IS A WOMAN'S WEAPON

AND A MAN'S EXCUSE.

—Henry Louis Mencken (humorous journalist
and critic of American life, 1880–1956)

WE ARE ALWAYS STRIVING FOR

THINGS FORBIDDEN, AND COVETING

THOSE DENIED US.

—Ovid (Roman poet, 43 B.C.–18 A.D.)

RESISTING TEMPTATION IS EASIER

WHEN YOU THINK YOU'LL PROBABLY

GET ANOTHER CHANCE LATER ON.

—Author Unknown

THERE ARE SEVERAL GOOD

PROTECTIONS AGAINST TEMPTATIONS,

BUT THE SUREST IS COWARDICE.

—Mark Twain (American humorist,
writer and lecturer, 1835–1910)

Do NOT BITE AT THE BAIT OF

PLEASURE 'TILL YOU KNOW THERE

IS NO HOOK BENEATH IT.

—Thomas Jefferson (American diplomat,
scholar and third U.S. President, 1743–1826)

I GENERALLY AVOID TEMPTATION

UNLESS I CAN'T RESIST IT.

—Mae West (American actress and
sex symbol, 1892–1980)

'TIS ONE THING TO BE TEMPTED,

ANOTHER THING TO FALL.

—William Shakespeare (English poet
and playwright, 1564–1616)

We MUST LEARN TO DO MORE WITH TEMPTATION

THAN JUST BEAR IT—WE MUST LEARN TO USE IT.

THE SECRET OF USING TEMPTATION, AND

TURNING IT TO OUR ADVANTAGE,

IS ONE OF LIFE'S GREATEST SECRETS.

—Selwyn Hughes
(Welsh author and preacher)

WHEN YOU ARE TEMPTED TO LOOK ELSEWHERE

FOR GREENER PASTURES, JUST REMEMBER SOMEONE

ELSE IS PROBABLY LOOKING AT YOURS. AND IF ANOTHER

PASTURE LOOKS GREENER, PERHAPS IT IS GETTING

BETTER CARE AND ATTENTION. GRASS IS ALWAYS

GREENER WHERE IT IS WATERED.

—Ezra Taft Benson (13th president of the
Church of Latter-Day Saints, 1899–1994)

EVERYTHING TEMPTS THE WOMAN

WHO FEARS TEMPTATION.

—French proverb

Most people want to be delivered

from temptation, but would

like it to keep in touch.

—Robert Orben (American writer
and humorist, b. 1927)

OPPORTUNITY MAY KNOCK ONLY ONCE,

BUT TEMPTATION LEANS ON THE DOORBELL.

—Author Unknown

THERE IS NOT ANY MEMORY RECALLED

WITH LESS SATISFACTION THAN THE MEMORY

OF SOME TEMPTATION WE RESISTED.

—James Branch Cabell (American essayist
and novelist, 1879–1958)

THE DEVIL TEMPTS US NOT—

'TIS WE TEMPT HIM, RECKONING HIS

SKILL WITH OPPORTUNITY.

—George Eliot
(English novelist, 1819–1880)

LEAD US NOT INTO TEMPTATION.

JUST TELL US WHERE IT IS,

WE'LL FIND IT.

—Samuel Levenson (American author
and humorist, 1911–1980)

DON'T WORRY ABOUT AVOIDING

TEMPTATION—AS YOU GROW OLDER,

IT STARTS AVOIDING YOU.

—Author Unknown

WHAT MAKES RESISTING TEMPTATION

DIFFICULT FOR MANY PEOPLE IS

THAT THEY DON'T WANT TO

DISCOURAGE IT COMPLETELY.

—Benjamin Franklin
(American statesman, 1706–1790)

THE ONLY WAY TO GET RID OF A TEMPTATION

IS TO YIELD TO IT. RESIST IT, AND YOUR SOUL

GROWS SICK WITH LONGING FOR THE

THINGS IT HAS FORBIDDEN TO ITSELF.

—Oscar Wilde,
The Picture of Dorian Gray, 1891

JUST THINK OF ALL THOSE WOMEN ON THE

TITANIC WHO SAID, 'NO, THANK YOU,'

TO DESSERT THAT NIGHT. AND FOR WHAT!

—Erma Bombeck (American humorist
and journalist, 1927–1996)

THE BEST WAY TO BEHAVE

IS TO MISBEHAVE.

—Mae West (American actress and
sex symbol, 1892–1980)

ONE CAN FIND WOMEN WHO HAVE NEVER

HAD ONE LOVE AFFAIR, BUT IT IS

RARE INDEED TO FIND ANY WHO

HAVE HAD ONLY ONE.

—Françoise de la Rochefoucauld (French classical author,
leading exponent of the Maxime, 1613–1680)

Here's a rule I recommend:

Never practice two vices at once.

—Tallulah Bankhead
(American actress, 1903–1968)

THE REAL ART OF CONVERSATION IS

NOT ONLY TO SAY THE RIGHT THING AT THE

RIGHT PLACE BUT TO LEAVE UNSAID THE

WRONG THING AT THE TEMPTING MOMENT.

—Dorothy Nevill
(British writer, 1826–1913)

MOST WOMEN HAVE SMALL WAISTS THE

WORLD THROUGHOUT, BUT THEIR DESIRES

ARE A THOUSAND MILES ABOUT.

— Cyril Tourneur
(English poet, 1575?–1626)

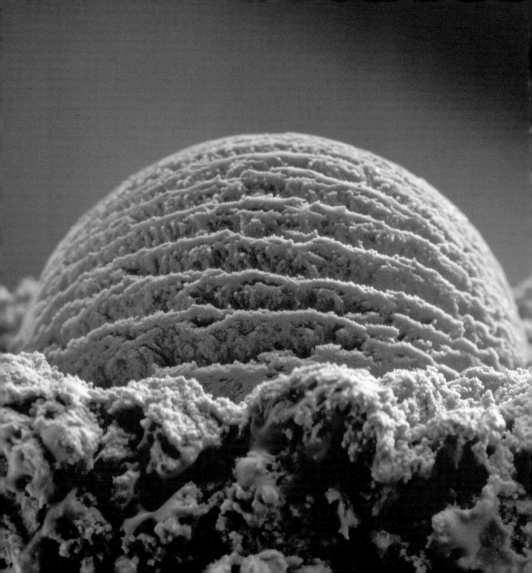

ALL WOMEN'S DRESSES, IN EVERY AGE AND COUNTRY,

ARE MERELY VARIATIONS ON THE ETERNAL

STRUGGLE BETWEEN THE ADMITTED DESIRE TO DRESS

AND THE UN-ADMITTED DESIRE TO UNDRESS.

—Lyn Yutang (Chinese writer and editor, 1895–1976)

WHEN A WOMAN WANTS A MAN AND

LUSTS AFTER HIM, THE LOVER NEED NOT BOTHER

TO CONJURE UP OPPORTUNITIES, FOR SHE

WILL FIND MORE IN AN HOUR THAN WE MEN

COULD THINK OF IN A CENTURY.

—Author Unknown

THERE IS GOOD SEX AND

THERE IS BAD SEX, BUT CHOCOLATE

IS ALWAYS CHOCOLATE.

—Author Unknown

THERE ARE TWO KINDS OF WOMEN:

THOSE WHO WANT POWER IN THE WORLD,

AND THOSE WHO WANT POWER IN BED.

—Jacqueline Kennedy Onassis
(1929–1994)

Abstinence makes the

heart grow fonder...

for someone else.

—Author Unknown

PHOTO CREDITS

COVER IMAGE: Rick Lew; P. 5: Mary Ellen Bartley; P. 6: Luca Trovato; P. 9: Mark Thomas; P. 10: Burke/ Triolo Productions; P. 13: Thomas Firak; P. 14: Richard Jung; P. 17: Paul Poplis; P. 18: John Blais; P. 21: Rick Lew; P. 22: Jeff Oshiro; P. 25: Sang An; P. 26: Rob Fiocca; P. 29: James Baigrie; P. 30: Melanie Acevedo; P. 33: Dennis Gottlieb; P. 34: Lew Robertson; P. 37: Evan Sklar; P. 38: Leigh Beisch;P. 41: Alan Richardson; P. 42: Lew Robertson; P. 45: Eric Futran; P. 46: State of Mind; P. 49: Brian Leatart; P. 50: Brian Hagiwara; P. 53: Brian Hagiwara; P. 54: David Bishop; P. 57: Steven Mark Needham; P. 58: Steven Mark Needham; P. 61: Steven Mark Needham; P. 62: Thomas Eckerle; P. 65: Joyce Oudkerk Pool, P. 66: Paul Poplis; P. 69: Rusty Hill; P. 70: Brian Hagiwara; P. 73: Burke/Triolo Productions; P. 74: John Svoboda; P. 77: Martin Jacobs; P. 78: David Bishop; P. 81: Intuitive Images Ltd.; P. 82: Matt Bowman; P. 85: Matt Bowman; P. 86: Burke/Triolo Productions

The beautiful photos you see throughout this book are courtesy of Jupiterimages.
For more information on the contributing photographers, visit www.jupiterimages.com.

jupiterimages.